101

EDUCATIONAL

VITO PERRONE

Teaching Curriculum, and
Learning Environments Chair
at HARVARD UNIVERSITY

CHELSEA HOUSE PUBLISHERS

New York • Philadelphia

CONVERSATIONS

With Your Kindergartner– 1st Grader

3 5 7 9 8 6 4 2

Library of Congress Cataloging-in-Publication Data

Perrone, Vito.
101 educational conversations with your kindergartner–first grader / Vito Perrone.
p. cm.
Includes bibliographical references and index.
  ISBN 0-7910-1918-7
      0-7910-1981-0 (pbk.)
1. Early childhood education—United States—Parent participation. 2. Parent and child—United States. 3. Communication—United States. I. Title. II. Title: One hundred one educational conversations you should have with your kindergartner–first grader. III. Title: One hundred and one educational conversations you should have with your kindergartner–first grader.
370.19'3—dc20   92-10795
                                                              CIP

Cover photo: Mark Ferri

CONTENTS

Other titles in the 101 EDUCATIONAL CONVERSATIONS *series:*

Unlike most countries, the United States does not have a formal national curriculum. In theory, each of the 15,000 school districts in the United States creates—with direction from state education agencies—its own curriculum. In practice, however, there are more similarities than differences among these curricula. What amounts to a national curriculum has been created through years of curriculum development by various national organizations related to the various subject areas, through the widespread use of textbooks prepared for a national market, and through standardized testing programs that are national in scope and are designed that the performance of children in any grade can be compared to the performance of children in the same grade but in a different community or state.

As a result of these standardizing forces, children in North Dakota study much the same subjects in their social studies classes, for example, as students in Massachusetts and Washington. They study their neighborhoods in grades 1 and 2, their cities in grade 3, their states in grade 4, American history in grade 5, some form of world history in grade 6, Latin America and Canada in grade 7, American history in grade 8, civics or world history in grade 9, global history or American history in grade 10, American history in grade 11, and either American government and economics or an elective course in American history or world history in grade 12.

The science curriculum becomes somewhat standardized in grade 9 with the study of physical science or earth science. High school students study biology in grade 10, chemistry in grade 11, and either physics or an elective course in biology or physical science in grade 12. In mathematics they study algebra I in grade 9, geometry in grade 10, algebra II in grade 11, and either trigonometry and precalculus or calculus in grade 12.

Each volume in the *101 Educational Conversations You Should Have with Your Child* series contains an outline of the typical curriculum for that particular grade. But you will probably find it helpful to ask your child's teacher about the curriculum for each new grade your child enters. The teacher can give you a fuller account of what is being taught in your school system.

You and Your Child's Education

Welcome to *101 Educational Conversations with Your Kinder-gartner–First Grader,* one of a series of books for parents who wish to be more involved in their children's education. I have written these books with two important goals in mind—first, to give parents a solid basis for talking with their children about their school experiences and thereby gaining further insight into their children's growth as learners; and second, to guide parents toward constructive, educa-tion-oriented interaction with teachers and administrators in their children's schools.

In my 30 years of experience in and around schools, I have found that parents are not always clear about what their children are learning in school, about whether their children's overall education is powerful or trivial, challenging or dull. Further, parents often lack a vision of what the schools—at their best—should provide students. It needs to be acknowledged, of course, that not all of what children must ultimately know and understand is learned in the schools. However, the schools do have an intentional curriculum, regardless of the grade level.

In the early years schools expect to teach children reading and writing, as well as certain aspects of science, social studies, and mathematics. They also expect to introduce children to the arts. These efforts should enable children not only to build upon what they learn at home but also to extend their classroom learning into the world outside school. Parents are a vital part of this endeavor. The more you know about the school's intentions and your child's responses, the better for your child's overall education.

Parents invariably ask their children, "What did you learn (or do) at school today?" and are treated to what has become the classic, predictable response: "Nothing." This is clearly a discouraging exchange, leaving parents on the outside or making them feel that they must press their children for details. But a parent's insistence only makes the exchange rather unnatural or even negative, with problematic results. Not only does the parent gain few new insights into the child's education, but the child may come to resent what he or she perceives as a grilling or as a routine, meaningless inquiry. The *101 Educational Conversations You Should Have with Your Child* series is designed to help parents get closer to what their children are learning. It encourages parents to find out what their children understand and also what they do not yet understand. The goal is to make parents' ongoing exchanges with their children about school and learning more natural and enjoyable, a mutual treat rather than a mutual burden.

At various times in the school year, parents are invited to parent-teacher conferences, where they often hear a good deal about how their children are progressing in different learning areas. In most cases, however, parents bring too little to these meetings. Rather than being genuine conversations, the conferences are one-sided reports. Parents may leave these sessions satisfied enough; in my experience, though, few of them say that they are fully engaged by the process. The *101 Educational Conversations You Should Have with Your Child* series should contribute to constructive change. These books are tools with which you can inform yourself about what the schools hope to teach and what your children are learning. You should then be able to bring to the parent-teacher conferences some of your own insights and perspectives about your children's educational growth. You will also be able to pose more potent questions to your children's teachers. As a result, your interactions with teachers should become more interesting and more constructive. The children and the schools will surely benefit.

An important premise of this series is that parents are their children's *first* teachers and their most critically important partners in learning. While this may seem most obvious to parents when their children are in the early primary grades, it is vital for parents to remain involved throughout their children's school lives. This is not, I grant, always easy. For one thing, parents often do not really know what the schools are teaching. In this regard the schools should be expected to provide much better information. Weekly guides would not be too much to expect. Nor would occasional workshops to give parents a fuller understanding of the questions children are asked in school, the books children read, and the principal objectives of the curriculum. If the schools do not deliver this kind of information to parents, then parents should ask, "Why not?"

Further, while schools typically say they value parent participation, parents are not always treated as full partners. This must change. If the schools do not actively acknowledge and encourage a strong role for parents, then parents themselves should take the initiative. Although this book is most concerned with the parent-child exchange, it will not have succeeded if it does not also empower parents in their relationships with their children's schools and teachers. In the end, the educational partnerships that we so desperately need—between parents and their children and between parents and schools—will be stronger.

101 Educational Conversations with Your Kindergartner–First Grader focuses on three areas of interest to parents:

- An overview of kindergarten and the first grade, with a look at how classrooms are organized, the kinds of experiences that are offered to children in these grades, and the basic curriculum—the content of what is taught.

- A collection of conversation starters and suggested activities—a how-to guide for parents who want to explore and expand their children's learning process through creative, stress-free interactions.

- A parent's guide to interacting with teachers and school administrators.

I wish to make one last point in this introduction. In the course of a school year, children study across many fields of inquiry. They read numerous books, view large numbers of films and videos, respond to many hundreds of questions, hear about a myriad of individuals and groups, explore the geography and politics of many countries, and learn many small facts and some larger conceptions. This book, and the others in this series, cannot cover *all* the ground that a child covers in a year. The most it can offer is a variety of useful places to begin. I expect that, once given these important guideposts, parents will be able to develop their own conversations and activities to enhance their understanding of their children's education while in turn enlarging the educational possibilities for the children. I trust that all of you who read this and the other books in the *101 Educational Conversations You Should Have with Your Child* series will have as good a time using the ideas as I and my colleagues have had in putting them together.

Your Child's Classroom

The best kindergarten and first grade classrooms are *developmentally appropriate*. This means that most activities are based on the physical, intellectual, social, and emotional development of each child, not on the children's ages or grade levels. Some children, for example, are ready for reading at age five; others reach this point when they are six or seven. Expecting all children to be at the same point, and teaching as if they are, not only limits the learning experience for many children but also induces feelings of failure that will not easily be overcome. Attention to individual development rather than emphasis on grade levels is especially important.

Developmentally appropriate classrooms are characterized by certain features. Among the most important of these are:

Respect for the Children

- Children's interests are important starting points for learning.

- Children's ideas and work are taken seriously.

- Children are understood to be actively in search of knowledge. Their play, questions, constructions, and speech are seen as part of the process of building knowledge.

- Children do as much talking as the teachers, or more.

- Children have many opportunities to choose—the stories they read, the projects they do, the activities they participate in.

- Children have *time* to observe, look around, wonder, and dream.

- Children work cooperatively, helping each other.

- Individual, racial, linguistic, and cultural differences are celebrated. They are seen as ways of enriching the children's lives.

Stimulation of Thought, Imagination, and Self-esteem

- Teachers respond to children's ideas and questions in ways that extend their learning rather than with rote answers.

- Teachers (and children) ask more open-ended questions than yes-or-no questions. Teachers spark exchanges by saying, "What if we did it this way?" "How else could we do it?" "Who has thought of another way?"

- Considerable attention is given to the processes of exploration and discovery, inquiry and investigation.

- Errors are seen as steps toward further learning, as particular inventions—not as mistakes or failures. Teachers respond to errors in ways that keep children's self-esteem intact and leave them eager to learn, not fearful of making a mistake.

- Teachers encourage risk taking and provide a safe, supportive environment for it.

An Abundance of Chances To Learn

- All forms of communication are given attention: reading, writing, listening, speaking. The classroom is full of language.

- The classroom is inviting and colorful, with a variety of interesting materials. The children know where these materials are kept and how to use them.

- Much of what is learned is rooted in real experiences, concrete materials, and hands-on activities. Teachers help the children make connections between the various areas of study. Knowledge is presented as an interconnected web, not as a handful of distinct categories that are unrelated to each other.

- Teachers keep learning, and they share what they learn with their students. They demonstrate that learning is a lifelong process and a source of delight.

- Children write their own books, which in turn can be read by others in the class. Moreover, functional print such as notes, letters, information, poems, and song lyrics are highly visible in the classroom.

- Children read real books by real authors, not just committee-produced "readers."

- Teachers know that learning takes place over time, and that children need numerous and related experiences before they are able to absorb critical concepts and use these concepts effectively as the basis of new learning.

- Evidence of interest in science and mathematics is highly visible.

Opportunities for Self-expression and Connections to the Children's Life Outside School

- Children have daily opportunities to participate in the creative and expressive arts: music, drawing, storytelling, drama.

- Children have daily opportunities to run, jump, and climb (extending the development of their large muscles) and to cut, paste, do puzzles, pound nails, and paint (for small-muscle development).

- Parents are welcome in the classroom. They are encouraged to be active participants in their children's education.

- Teachers make an effort to connect children's lives in school to experiences outside of school such as reading at home, getting a pet, taking a family vacation, eating a new food for the first time, seeing a movie with their parents, and the like.

Teachers who think in developmental terms understand that they can return often to a particular topic of study. Each time they do so, the children's levels of comprehension will have changed. I know of one first grade child who told his teacher, "If you put a piece of coal in a cup of water it will turn into a diamond." The child put a piece of coal in a cup of water, put it on his desk, and waited for his diamond. After a few days—during which no diamond appeared—the teacher asked the boy what he thought was happening to the coal. "How can we find out more about coal and diamonds?" the teacher said. Some children in the first grade, and certainly most children in the second and third grades, would immediately have dismissed the idea that coal can turn into a diamond. But the teacher, understanding that this child was at a different level of comprehension, respected the child's idea, enabled him to test it, and then guided him toward finding out for himself how coal turns into diamonds.

A teacher might ask children to sort rocks into different piles according to how the rocks look to the children. Most K–1 children will sort the rocks into two piles. When asked why they arranged them as they did, the children might say, "These are big and those are little" or "These are shiny and those are not." Some children, though, might have a third pile in which rocks are differentiated on the basis of color or shape or use. And by grade 3, all children will be able to work with several attributes at once. The concrete experiences along the way make a difference.

In developmental classrooms, teachers often build the curriculum around themes. For instance, the children may be studying dinosaurs—a popular topic among children everywhere. The children will read about dinosaurs, write about dinosaurs, research the size of the different dinosaurs and plot the information on a graph, sing songs about dinosaurs, make large papier-mâché dinosaurs, create their own poems about dinosaurs, and visit a museum where they can see models of dinosaurs. Because children at this age are just beginning to understand conceptions of size and length, they might be able to identify the *largest* dinosaur in a picture but not comprehend the meaning of its *25 feet of length* The teacher will not expect everyone to understand the concept of *25 feet*. But over time, after working with the idea of *length* in relation to many objects and spaces, all the children will come to understand it.

The Physical Environment

What are kindergarten and first grade classrooms like? At their best they are decentralized, with many diverse spaces organized for a variety of purposes. Instead of desks they often contain small moveable tables and chairs that can easily be arranged and rearranged. In those settings without desks each child will have a space, usually a box (or cubby), for his or her important belongings. These spaces are treated with great respect by the teacher and the children.

While teachers will organize the various learning spaces in their classrooms according to their own preferences, the arrangements described below are not uncommon. The description is of a classroom I especially like. It is a K–1 classroom, in which kindergarten and first grade children are integrated into a single class, and the room's features are applicable to either grade.

READING

The reading area is particularly inviting. It is brightly carpeted, with a rocking chair, several pillows on the floor, and many books and magazines that are freely accessible to the children. The reading materials cover a broad range of subjects and are geared to a broad range of ability levels. Among them are quite a few books written by the children themselves. On display are "ideas for sharing," "new books in the center," and "books I especially liked." Such descriptions are written by the children as well as by the teacher.

LANGUAGE ARTS

The language arts area is adjacent to the reading area. It contains materials and equipment relating to the whole spectrum of communications: pencils and paper, a typewriter, two computers, a tape recorder equipped with headsets, and tapes. Some of the tapes are music for the children's enjoyment; some are stories, occasionally associated with particular read-along books; and some are skill lessons in such areas as listening and writing. There is also a variety of reading and spelling games (most of them made by the teacher), puzzles, and a box containing pictures and ideas for writing. Poetry and stories created by the children are on display; so are new words and ways to use them.

SCIENCE

The science area is designed for active involvement with materials. It changes more often than most of the other learning centers in the room, and it generally contains more "common," noncommercial materials than the other centers. A variety of units from the Elementary Science Study ("small things," "peas and particles," "structures," "pendulums") are found here. These are open-ended study tools that give children experience in such processes as analyzing, classifying, measuring, and predicting. They employ balances, lenses, simple microscopes, magnets, prisms, thermometers, plastic tubing, bottles and jugs, containers with water and sand, candles, rocks, and shells. This particular science area also has a large incubator, small motors, nuts and bolts, and pulleys. And there are living things: an aquarium with a variety of water life and cages with hamsters. An electric frying pan is made available once a week for cooking projects. (Cooking produces enormous enthusiasm because everyone can be successful at it. In addition, it provides an excellent opportunity for integrating the various curriculum areas; in the course of planning a cooking project and following a recipe, children work with concepts from science, health, reading, and math.) The science area also holds primary science reference books on animals, plants, insects, rocks, astronomy, and engines. Projects that have been completed by individuals or groups of children are on display.

MATH

The math area also stresses active involvement with materials and thinking. Activities such as measuring, weighing, graphing, sorting, and classifying are encouraged. Tools to help children with these activities—tape measures, string, rulers, balances, and jars of various sizes—are at hand. There are also plenty of things to help children count and learn about geometric shapes: buttons, washers, abacuses, dice, Cuisenaire rods, multicolored and multishaped blocks, and tangrams (Chinese puzzles with geometric shapes that can be put together in a variety of different ways). There are math games, puzzles, flash cards, and work pages. Finally, the teacher has prepared a large number of "activity cards" that guide children toward sequential learning of some mathematical concepts.

DRAMA

The drama area serves a broad range of the expressive arts, from pantomime, role playing, and puppetry to some forms of movement and music. It contains a puppet theater, materials for making puppets, dress-up clothes, records and a record player, several recorders and drums, an autoharp, and a variety of rhythm instruments constructed by the children. Improvisation is strongly encouraged.

WOODWORKING

The woodworking area includes an old table that serves as a workbench. Hammers, saws, screwdrivers, pliers, nails, rulers, glue, wire, and sandpaper are stored on a pegboard or in plastic containers. Local lumberyards supply scraps of wood from which the children make boxes, boats, rockets, and geometric designs.

This particular classroom is a rich environment. Its wide range of learning materials—paints, brushes, wood, paper, scissors, batteries, masking tape, wire, audiotapes, filmstrips, and more—is easily accessible. The teacher considers it important that the children know what materials are available, where they are stored, and how to use them. Once the children have learned how to use tools and equipment safely, they have virtually complete access to all materials. The teacher knows that if children do not know what is available to them, or if they must ask permission to use the items (which usually involves waiting), they may lose interest, and their opportunities for exploration will be limited. It should be noted, too, that children in this classroom do things for themselves: they mix paints and clean brushes, and they operate tape recorders, filmstrip projectors, record players, and computers. These simple tasks are part of the process of learning self-reliance and responsibility.

ART

The art area contains three easels; together they can serve six children. It also contains such art supplies as aprons, paints (water and tempera), jars, brushes, many different kinds of paper, clay, chalk, scissors, and a variety of craft materials such as egg cartons, glue, string, vinyl tile, wood chips, yarn, wallpaper, and magazines. At times, because of the children's interests or activities, the art area also contains leaves, starch, Styrofoam, rubber, twigs, dyes, and looms.

What Parents Want to Know

One question that parents often ask about primary classrooms is, What should the class size be? Class size *is* important. Optimally, kindergarten and first grade classrooms should have no more than 16 to 20 children. These early years are fluid; children's levels of learning vary widely. The more individual attention teachers can provide, and the more experiences they can facilitate for each child, the better. But as class size goes beyond 20, the potential for individual interaction decreases.

In the previous chapter, I described a classroom rich in materials. My experience is that as class size reaches 24, 28, or 30 children— which is, unfortunately, the norm—the classroom becomes a less rich environment for each child. Teachers and parents need to become more vocal about the importance of class size in these early, most formative years.

Another question that comes up often is, How much homework is reasonable for K–1 children? Most teachers do not assign much formal homework during these early years, but *some* homework could be useful, especially if it is interesting, if it goes beyond the daily school activities, and if it can be done with a parent.

Homework assignments in kindergarten might include: See how many objects you can find in your house that are red, blue, or yellow. Tell a story to your mother or father. Count the doors or windows in your house. A first grader might receive these homework assignments: Read to your mother or father. Read for 20 minutes on your own. Think about "fairy tale" words. Practice printing letters. A first grader might also be expected to do some sorting and classifying exercises or computational exercises. But K–1 children should *not* have homework that takes more than 20 to 30 minutes. If their homework assignments exceed this limit, parents should inquire about it. And if there is *no* homework, that too is worth an inquiry.

I am also often asked whether children should be using computers in kindergarten or first grade. While many children are using computers at home at age five or six, and some schools have computers in K–1 classrooms, I do not view them as essential at this level. There is so much language to hear and use, so much to observe in the natural world, so much concrete experience to gain, that waiting until second or third grade for active computer use seems reasonable.

A Parents' Guide to Teachers' Terminology

As they become involved with their children's schools, parents will hear teachers use many special terms to describe what happens in the classroom. Some of the most important of these terms are explained below.

LEARNING STYLES
Children learn in many different ways, although each child has a preference for one or two particular ways of learning. These preferences are called *learning styles*. Some children learn most easily when ideas, concepts, and information are first presented visually, through pictures or videos. Others gain understanding only after firsthand

work such as writing, experimenting, problem solving, or playacting. Some children need to have ideas presented in a very precise and sequential order; for others close attention to sequence complicates learning rather than promoting it. Teachers are most effective when they know children well enough to understand their individual learning styles. This lets them individualize each child's learning experiences.

INVENTIVE OR TRANSITIONAL SPELLING

Teachers typically get children started writing in kindergarten. If children had to concentrate on correct spelling in kindergarten and first grade, however, they would do very little significant writing. Spelling is the last of the teacher's concerns as a child's writing moves from scribbles and pictures to actual letters. "The bebe is hape" (the baby is happy) has to be seen as a wonderful piece of early writing.

The period of transition from inventive spelling to traditional spelling is generally about two to three years. By the end of the second grade, certainly in the third grade, most children are well along in conventional spelling. But pushing them there too soon will likely diminish them as writers.

In the transitional period, teachers will send notes to children using correct spelling *without* stressing the difference. For instance, a first grade child's entry in her writing journal might be: "I hve a cat. He ets gras. I lik him." The teacher's response would be: "It is funny to see a cat eat grass. I wish my cat would eat grass. I like my cat. He drinks milk and eats cat food. What color is your cat? What other funny things does your cat do?" Notice that the teacher's response spells *have, grass, eat,* and *like* correctly, while accepting the child's work as it was written. The teacher also invites the child to write more about her cat.

BASAL READERS

Basal readers are textbooks designed to teach reading in a sequential, skill-oriented way. They are generally accompanied by numerous prepackaged materials, including workbooks. The stories included in the basal readers have controlled vocabularies, going from what are viewed as easier words to more complex words, from very short sentences of three words to longer sentences of four to six words, and the like. Most schools use basal readers, although if they are rigidly followed they do not match the principles of developmentally appropriate classrooms.

Some children, for example, need much more experience with language—hearing more language in more contexts, talking more, seeing more printed letters and words—before they can effectively start the basal series in reading. But the basal program assumes that all children of the same age start from the same point. Because everything in the program is sequential, those who have less language experience when they start the program are automatically behind as readers. Young children do not need this kind of negative beginning. On the other hand, the basal program may have first grade children studying such vocabulary words as *and, in, the, up,* and *away*—but some of these children are already reading *Charlotte's Web* at home. These more developed readers are not being challenged or helped much by the basal reading program.

LITERATURE-BASED READING PROGRAMS

Literature-based reading programs, often called "whole language programs," take an approach to reading different from the basal program. In a literature-based program, children read real books by identified authors—books such as Eric Carle's *The Hungry Caterpillar* and Beatrix Potter's *Peter Rabbit*. A classroom using this approach to reading will have many books, on a variety of topics and at many levels of complexity. Some will be easy to read, with pictures telling most of the story, and others will be more difficult. The children make choices about which books they read. A growing number of teachers believe that literature-based reading programs not only are more appropriate developmentally than skill-based basal reading programs but make the children more effective as readers and writers.

PHONICS

Phonics is a system of teaching children to read by sounding out individual letters. For example, a child might read the word *book* by sounding out the *b*, the *oo*, and the *k*: "buh," "oo," "kuh"—"book." The role of phonics in reading programs has become a subject of highly charged debate. Proponents of phonics argue that it is the key to reading; others suggest that it bears little important relation to reading and wastes children's time. I do not view phonics as an either-or proposition. Many children—but not all of them—are likely to benefit from some attention to phonics. It will be useful to them to know how to use sounds as a way to deal with unfamiliar words, although they should also be encouraged to try other methods of approaching new words, such as the context in which the word appears or its similarity to other words. Regardless of the method they use to teach reading, the most effective teachers will introduce phonics quite naturally within the context of their work with language, even as they understand that turning phonics into a separate activity is not a particularly constructive use of time.

DISCOVERY LEARNING

In classrooms organized around discovery learning, children are encouraged to ask questions, investigate subjects that interest them, and find solutions to problems. Teachers tend not to provide answers but rather help children seek their own answers. Teachers encourage questions by raising questions themselves, by filling the classrooms with interesting materials, and by drawing upon many of the children's own experiences.

Suppose a child wants to know more about a particular animal. The teacher might ask the child what ideas he or she already has about finding the information and then suggest additional avenues for exploration. The conversation might go like this:

TEACHER: How could you determine what kind of animal that is?

CHILD: Read, look in the encyclopedia, find it in the animal book, ask my dad.

TEACHER: If you used the encyclopedia, what book would you go to?

CHILD: I don't know.

TEACHER: Let's think of some way we could decide which book to use.

Here are other examples of the kind of exchange that is heard in discovery-based classrooms:

TEACHER: How would you know how many balls it would take to fill up this cylinder?

CHILD: Let's fill the cylinder with the balls and count them.

TEACHER: That is one way. Let's do that, but then let's see if we can figure out any other ways.

CHILD: How do you draw a horse?

TEACHER: If you did know, where would you start?

CHILD: At the head. I'll try it.

The teacher's role in the discovery-based classroom is to help children find many of their own solutions by giving them a framework for asking and answering questions. Essentially, the teacher introduces children to new ways of thinking.

ASSESSMENT

Assessment refers to the measuring of children's progress. More and more educational professionals, at least those involved in early childhood education, believe that we should stop relying on traditional standardized tests, which evaluate children on the basis of fixed standards of skill, achievement, or intelligence. Children's growth is most uneven in kindergarten and first grade. In the early years, children are acquiring the skills they will need for success in school, and these skills are in a fluid, ever-changing state. Teachers should not make judgments that contribute to failure by attaching negative labels or by separating children into "good," "average," or "slow learner" groups. Standardized tests, however, often imply and contribute such labels or separations.

More and more schools are ending all standardized testing in the early grades, K–1 in particular. Instead, teachers assess students by keeping ongoing records of performance, documenting students' work on a day-by-day basis. Teachers also keep portfolios of children's work; these are available for parents to review.

COOPERATIVE LEARNING

Cooperative learning is a means of helping children work together in order to enlarge their learning. Cooperative learning groups are organized to work on projects together, solve mathematics and science problems, do experiments, share stories, read to each other, and the like. In kindergarten and the first grade, a buddy system, or groups of two children working together, is particularly effective.

BALANCE

Teachers in the early grades, especially those who lean toward developmentally appropriate teaching, talk a good deal about the need for balance. Balance means quiet times followed by active times followed by quiet times; times when children work alone and times when they work with others; times for physical activity and times for activities directed toward social and emotional development; times to explore and times to consolidate learning. The days must be varied and should address the needs of the "whole child."

THE TEACHER AS FACILITATOR

A facilitator is someone who makes it easier for another to do something. Teachers who guide, question, and support children in their learning are facilitators; they make it easier for children to learn, but they give the central role in the learning process to the children themselves. Teachers who see themselves as facilitators stimulate children and challenge them to think and question. They provide a diversity of materials and activities, and they search for new books and questions that will extend children's learning and enlarge their awareness. They spend much of their time supporting children's investigations. In contrast, teachers who "give answers" most of the time and who do most of the talking in a classroom are not facilitators.

Your Child's School Day

What is your child's school day like? Although each teacher will organize his or her class somewhat differently, what follows is the typical daily schedule of a K–1 classroom that I enjoy visiting.

8:30–9:00 A.M.

The classroom is open when the first child arrives in the morning. The teacher greets the children as they come in and helps them get involved in interesting activities. They may, for example, sit quietly with another child and visit, begin reading, start writing a story, build with the blocks, or listen to a story on the tape recorder. Essentially, this is a time for everyone to get comfortable with the beginning of another school day.

9:00–10:00 A.M.

The children gather for the formal opening activity. The teacher usually begins with the news of the day: birthdays, visitors, new materials, or special events. This is followed by announcements the children wish to make, perhaps about something they want to show, something interesting they have observed, a new word or song they have learned, or a funny or "scary" experience. After these announcements, the teacher reads a story. She then records on charts what everyone is planning to do during the day and what groups she will call together for particular activities. As she prepares the charts, she may point out how she has used periods, question marks, and capital letters. She will also call the children's attention to some of the new words she has used.

10:15–10:35 A.M.
Everyone (including the teacher) selects a book and reads quietly.

10:35–11:30 A.M.
Children carry out their plans for the morning. The teacher guides and challenges the children, carrying out her role as a facilitator of learning. During this time she also has a lot of individual conferences with students.

11:30 A.M.–Noon
The children gather for a story. This provides them with some quiet time during which their energies are focused on listening and thinking. The teacher may encourage the children to think about and discuss the story by asking questions: "If there were five children in the family instead of one, how would it have been different?" "How could we change the ending of the story?" "What other characters would we need if we changed the ending of the story?"

Noon–12:40 P.M.
Break time for lunch and outdoor play.

12:40–1:00 P.M.
Gathering time and planning time. The teacher guides the children through such questions as "What do I have left to finish before I go

home?" "What questions do I have?" "Have I completed work in the math area, the science area?" "Have I read a book?" "What project am I working on?" "How long will I need to finish my project?"

1:00–2:10 P.M.

Large block of time to work. The teacher circulates, questions, gathers small groups of children together to work on various skills as needed, and gives support and encouragement to the children as they proceed with their activities.

2:10–2:25 P.M.

Break time, often outside play time. (Some of the younger children rest.)

2:25–3:00 P.M.

Sustained Silent Writing (SSW) and Writer's Workshops. Children learn to put the ideas they have in their heads onto paper. For kindergarten children, the first stage might be to dictate a story to the teacher and then draw a picture representing the ideas in the story. As these children progress, their work might incorporate many sentences about their ideas and understandings, making full use of invented or transitional spelling. Every child writes or finds a way to express himself or herself in writing, especially during this time but also at other times of the school day.

3:00–3:30 P.M.

The children show or share some of the things they have been working on. They add finished work to their folders. They put things that they are still working on into their working files, all ready for the next day. During this time they reflect on the day's activities. The teacher may encourage them to ask themselves, Which of the activities was most interesting? What will I work on tomorrow? What am I going to tell my parents about tonight? What book will I read at home?

3:30–3:40 P.M.

Gradual dismissal, with good-byes to everyone.

What Your Child Learns in School

This chapter is an overview of the typical curriculum for kindergarten and first grade, intended to give you an idea of what your child is learning. But because children learn in different ways and at different rates, not all children will grasp a particular part of the curriculum at the same time. While most kindergarten children will master what is outlined below as the common kindergarten curriculum, others will need another year to solidify their understanding of some subjects. Teachers and parents who understand development, who do not view the curriculum in terms of rigid grades or steps, will accept this as quite normal.

I distinguish between kindergarten and first grade in this overview, but the two levels should properly be viewed as connected and as overlapping at many points. And while I have divided the curriculum into different subject areas for convenience, in reality the boundaries between subject areas are blurred in these early years. Parents should also be aware that teaching in these early primary grades is more informal than formal. Much of what children learn comes through activities and concrete experiences rather than through a teacher imparting information.

One last point needs to be made about the curriculum. I have refrained from listing certain familiar and specific elements—standard children's rhymes such as "Little Bo-peep" and "Humpty Dumpty," traditional hero stories about George Washington, basic number facts such as 2+2=4. All of these have a place in the classroom. But teachers must bring a diverse and rich array of literature to children, introduce children to many people who make up the traditions of their communities and of the country, and involve children in the fullest use of mathematics. The teacher's primary responsibility is to ensure that children maintain a sense of curiosity, that they love reading and writing, and that they take an ongoing interest in the world around them. The teacher's job is to help children be active and confident learners.

In doing this job, teachers will likely make use of such traditional rhymes as "Humpty Dumpty." But they may find among the songs or stories relating to their children's cultural traditions a more interesting rhyme, something with greater potential to stimulate children's language development and enlarge their learning. Similarly, the traditional heroes and narratives of United States history will surely emerge in the classroom. Knowing that the traditional histories often excluded women and persons of color, however, teachers will take care to expose the children to other, less traditional heroes and narratives. And by counting and manipulating objects in a concrete way, children not only learn number facts of the 2+2=4 variety but also absorb the rules governing addition, subtraction, multiplication, and division.

The curriculum in the early primary grades should be rich and full of diverse starting points so that each child—with his or her individual interests, learning style, and level of development—can enter fully into the learning process. And the curriculum must always be intellectually challenging.

As I noted in the introduction, teachers should be expected to have clear goals for the children they teach. A teacher should be able to say what the children will understand, or be able to do, by the end of the school year, and to explain how everything he or she does in the classroom is related to those goals. Teachers should also be able to explain how they assess each child's progress toward those goals and how they will stay in touch with parents.

The Kindergarten Curriculum

LANGUAGE ARTS

Children's learning in the early primary grades is centered on language: reading, writing, listening, and speaking. Most other curriculum areas, in fact, grow out of this focus on language. Teachers understand that by the time they start school, virtually all children have learned to speak and listen (which are enormously complex skills). These skills are a strong base. Yet some children have had more experience with language than others. To ensure that rewarding language experiences are shared by everyone, teachers fill these early years with language, paying attention to the children's individual differences.

Reading

In the area of reading, the teacher's goals are that the children know that print is talk written down and that it can be read; know that writers of print are authors; become increasingly fond of books and literature (including stories, plays, song lyrics, poems, rhymes, and news stories) and of going to the library; learn to "read" pictures and signs; learn to read the names of colors and common objects in print; recognize the letters of the alphabet in both uppercase and lowercase; learn to differentiate between various sounds or letters; enlarge their vocabularies by hearing new words and engaging in new experiences; begin reading the stories they have dictated; begin reading stories with which they are familiar and begin building an awareness of how language works; and participate in Sustained Silent Reading.

Writing

Writing is an extension of reading. At the K–1 level the teacher's goals are that the children put marks on paper (scribbles at first); "write" through pictures, another early stage of story writing; become aware that everyone has ideas that can be turned into stories in print, perhaps by dictation to a teacher, older sibling, or parent; learn to form letters and numerals; begin to write words, using invented or transitional spelling; try to express ideas through print (it is important that parents and teachers applaud the inventiveness and creativity of beginning writers); learn that stories can be changed, expanded, reorganized, and even discarded if they do not work; participate in the writer's workshops; use writing at school and at home, in messages, invitations, lists, letters to friends, and thank-you letters.

Listening

Children have been listeners for a long time before they start kindergarten, but in school listening becomes a more conscious activity. The teacher's goals are that children take turns and let other speakers finish before they speak; interact with a speaker by responding to what they hear; listen purposefully to stories, records, tapes, sounds, and rhymes; practice conversation; listen to directions, report them, and follow them; listen to information and pass it along to others.

Speaking

As with listening, children have been speaking for some time before they start kindergarten. Because it is closely tied to all the other communication forms, speaking is a matter for study in kindergarten. The teacher's goals for children are that they take part in class discussions; participate in speaking activities such as show-and-tell, chants, songs, and plays; learn numerous nursery rhymes and poems through repetition; use the telephone as a means of learning to speak clearly; visit with friends at school and at home; interact with adults in school and at home.

MATHEMATICS

Concrete experiences are basic to the kindergarten math curriculum. At this early stage of schooling, math is as much about vocabulary as about numerals, and it is more concerned with consolidating understanding than with rote knowledge.

Basic Terms

Teachers want children to understand these basic terms used to describe relations among objects or numbers: more than, less than, the same as, different from, equal to, and group or set.

Spatial Terms

Children commonly work with these spatial terms: near and far, in and out, above and below, up and down, top and bottom, in front of and in back of, open and closed, right and left, to and from, empty and full, between, beside, across, first, next, and last.

Comparisons

Children commonly learn to use the following terms of comparison: tall and short; big and small; long and short; tall, taller, tallest; short, shorter, shortest; big, bigger, biggest; small, smaller, smallest; long, longer, longest.

Numerals

Most children arrive at kindergarten age with some experience in counting and some knowledge of numbers. At school they build on this base by learning to count to 20; to identify and write numerals up to 20; to order objects by first, second, third, fourth, and fifth; to match objects or sort them into groups by size or color; and to recognize that groups contain as many as five objects without having to count each object.

Shapes

The study of shapes is an entry into geometry. Kindergarten children begin that study by learning to recognize circles, squares, rectangles, and triangles.

Time, Money, and Measurement

Teachers' goals in the areas of time, money, and measurement are that children tell time to the hour; understand such concepts as morning, afternoon, day, noon, and night; identify coins (penny, nickel, dime, quarter) and have some understanding of their value; learn to estimate distances as well as measure them informally with string, with their hands and feet, or with other imaginative contrivances; and identify differences in the size and weight of objects.

SCIENCE

Young children are naturally curious and inquisitive, always delighted to explore the world around them. The main role of the science curriculum in kindergarten is to support and encourage this curiosity.

Living Things

Children explore the nature of plants and animals—their growth patterns, their uses, and the care they require. Children learn to describe and care for plants and animals, recording their findings in science journals through pictures, dictation, or kindergarten-style writing.

The Five Senses

Children make conscious use of tasting, smelling, hearing, touching, and seeing to gain information about the world.

Development of Inquiry and Thinking Skills

Children learn how to observe carefully, to question, and to conduct small experiments (typically with plants and animals).

HEALTH

Kindergarten children engage in physical activities that are related to both gross motor development (running, jumping, climbing) and fine motor development (puzzles, blocks, balancing games). They learn about some aspects of growth and development. Much of the science curriculum is related to health, and so are some of the stories in the language arts curriculum.

Basic Health Habits

Children learn the importance of caring for their bodies: teeth, eyes, physical exercise, rest, and cleanliness. Well-being is emphasized.

Nutrition

Children learn about the food groups, the importance of food choices and good eating habits, the values of different foods, and the eating customs of various cultures.

Safety

Safety training for kindergarten children stresses the importance of being careful around machinery, in the streets, and on the layground. It also covers fire prevention, the use of the 911 number, and awareness of poisons.

SOCIAL STUDIES

In the earliest years of school, the social studies curriculum is oriented toward the family and the neighborhood, social relationships, and what might be called civic responsibilities. The social studies curriculum is also intended to give children the basis for interacting with and understanding people of other cultures, as well as the foundation for later studies in history and geography. The teacher's goals for the children are that they recognize their names in print; know their telephone numbers and how to use the telephone; know their street addresses; name all the people in their families and extended families and know what each family member does and enjoys; describe how they get to school and map the route; describe their favorite things, friends, and activities; understand and appreciate the different kinds of families that exist (two parents, a single parent, stepparents, and the like); begin to know something about families in other cultures; begin to know the significance of civic and religious holidays, both their own and those of other people; begin to learn about such national historical figures as George Washington, Benjamin Franklin, George Washington Carver, Thomas Jefferson, Harriet Beecher Stowe, Abraham Lincoln, Frederick Douglass, Chief Joseph, Elizabeth Cady Stanton, Sojourner Truth, and Martin Luther King, Jr.; become familiar with such principles of citizenship as being responsible for their own actions, helping to make group decisions, sharing, and respecting others; and start studying geography through such subjects as weather, seasons, and maps.

THE ARTS

Self-expression is natural to young children and should be supported and encouraged. It is important that both teachers and parents accept children's artistic expressions uncritically. The focus of the arts curriculum in the early years is enjoyment.

Music

Children sing, experiment with making sounds using a variety of rhythm instruments, listen to many different kinds of music, compose songs, and attend musical performances.

Movement

Children use their bodies in creative dance and view dance performances.

Drama
Children use puppets, play dress-up, put on plays, and view performances of plays.

Drawing and Sculpture
Children experiment with various media such as tempera paints, crayons, pencils, markers, and clay. They also observe and discuss artwork in museums, libraries, and parks.

Poetry and Creative Writing
Children create poems, songs, stories, and plays. The works of individual children or of groups are collected into books.

The First Grade Curriculum

In many respects, the first grade curriculum is an extension of what children have begun in kindergarten. In terms of curriculum, the child's experience of first grade has (and should have) more in common with kindergarten than it will have with second grade. Some first grade work, however, is more structured and sequential than was the case in kindergarten. Further, reading and writing will become more focused on curriculum subjects. But, at least in the best of settings, learning is not yet compartmentalized into distinct subject areas.

Below I describe some of the elements that are added to the curriculum in the first grade. You should assume that most of what was outlined earlier in the kindergarten curriculum extends into first grade classrooms and overlaps this new material.

LISTENING AND SPEAKING

The oral aspects of language continue to be seen as important. Children listen to *more* stories, but the stories are also more complex and feature greater intensity of human feeling. First grade children also expand their vocabularies; do more retelling of the stories they hear (this helps them to understand the stories' logic in terms of beginnings, middles, and ends); identify rhyming patterns; create mental images of what they hear and describe these images; discriminate more fully among sounds; discuss differences in intensity of words and sounds; speak about their ideas; take part in conversations and discussions; learn to take messages and pass them on; and learn an increasing array of nursery rhymes, poems, chants, and songs, with many opportunities to "perform" what they have learned.

READING AND WRITING

Teachers want children to *enjoy* reading and writing, not just know how to read and write. First grade children continue to work on sound-to-letter connections; they also begin identifying prefixes and suffixes. But the emphasis shifts from reading as mastery of letters and words to reading as a way of getting to the meaning of a text. Children keep journals of words they know, regularly adding new words. Simple books with predictable patterns—familiar stories or stories with clues in the pictures—are introduced, and there are *many* books for children to choose from. Children are taught to "pass over" words they do not know and keep going, or to infer the meaning of words from the context or the pictures; these methods keep them from losing interest or becoming discouraged. Children are encouraged to keep the story flowing with their own inventions. Teachers also equip children with strategies for sounding out words they do not know. First grade teachers do more reading with small groups of children. This allows the teacher to introduce new information, to help children with new words and meanings, and to hear children read aloud. Such groups, though, are never permanent and are *not* labeled in a judgmental way, such as "high, middle, and low" reading groups. Labels that create castes among the children are not helpful.

Writing continues to be closely related to reading. The volume of writing increases steadily through grade 1. Children are encouraged to get their ideas on paper, spelling the words as they sound to them, and to think of themselves as *real* authors. They write more to each other, to the teacher, to their parents, and to classroom visitors; they produce an increasing number of books to enlarge their sense of authorship; and they begin to recognize authorship in what they read. They are also encouraged to find favorites among children's authors.

MATHEMATICS

As in kindergarten, mathematics in grade 1 is more concrete than abstract. Children's work consists not of hundreds of worksheets with problems such as 2+2=__ but of manipulating buttons and other objects, seeing patterns, and understanding the various uses of quantitative concepts. In this sense children use math in the course of working with science, cooking, health, social studies, reading, and writing. In more traditional terms, they count and write numbers on an ever-increasing scale, from 20 to 30, from 30 to 40, and so on. Their concepts of order expand from fifth to sixth and on to twelfth; they use such symbols as +, -, =, <, and >; they gain a firmer grasp of addition and subtraction; they begin solving "story" problems (written problems that relate as much as possible to children's experiences); they do more work with shapes and segments of shapes; they are introduced to the concepts of whole, half, and quarter; they master time telling to the half hour, if not to the minute; they gain a fuller sense of historical time; they use standard measures such as cup, pint, and teaspoon. They learn to estimate: How many seeds are in a pumpkin? Does the size of the pumpkin make a difference? How much difference? They move from these estimates to estimates of length and distance, and they make graphs of their estimates and measurements. As a result of this varied approach to math, children come to see the mathematics involved in buildings and bridges, in quilts, in buying the right amount of wallpaper, in knowing how much money they must save to buy a particular toy or a radio.

SCIENCE

Exploration of the natural world continues to be an important area of study. The teacher fosters curiosity and imparts the tools of inquiry, so that children readily ask, "Why is that?" "How does that happen?" "What if—?" Children learn to focus their inquiries within a subject. The investigation of insects, for example, might involve examining their characteristics, observing their activities, learning to recognize different varieties, and noting differences and similarities; another common and fully engaging activity is following the stages of a butterfly's development. (Plants and animals are always interesting because they are living things and because children can see plants and animals in the world around them.) A more abstract focus of investigation might be weather, including the seasons, cloud structures, the sun and the moon, and temperature. The study of magnets allows children to develop techniques of experimentation.

HEALTH

Children continue to learn about their bodies—for example, "What happens when I lose my teeth?" They also participate in and enjoy a variety of physical activities; learn how to describe pain and symptoms of illness; continue to gain understanding of nutrition and the importance of promoting health; learn about drugs and their effects; learn something about the sources of food; examine safety rules—for the playground, automobiles, and the street as well as fire safety rules—and learn something about the purpose of each rule; meet professional health workers; study growth and development by graphing their own growth and by observing the growth of plants and animals; observe babies and young children; meet with older people.

SOCIAL STUDIES

Learning about families and neighborhoods is an essential part of social studies throughout the primary grades, even as children learn about other parts of the United States and the world. In the first grade, children learn more about families and how they live and work, in the United States and elsewhere; explore aspects of the economy such as jobs, transportation, stores and shops, income, spending, and saving; study the different cultures in their region; begin to learn the concepts of city, state, and nation; practice democratic processes such as making rules and decisions; learn inquiry skills such as becoming aware of a problem, knowing how to gain information, being able to organize and analyze information, and finding solutions. They advance their study of geography by learning the four main directions and using maps. History becomes more important at this level; a common focus of study is how children lived in other times. Children are encouraged to hear stories of their parents' and grandparents' childhoods. "Once upon a time" and "long ago, in a faraway land" are the openings of some fascinating stories that are read to children to give them a sense of historical thinking.

THE ARTS

In the early years, children are encouraged to express themselves in all the arts, to create landscapes, sound, music, and symbolic language. As children gain greater control of crayons and brushes, and as their eye-hand coordination improves, their drawings and paintings will become more detailed and colorful. In grade 1 children will become more conscious of the aesthetic character of their classroom and the school; they will organize plays; and they will become more skillful in the use of rhythm instruments.

Children gain a great deal—in terms of self-esteem, expressiveness, and sheer pleasure—from being active in as many of the arts as possible throughout their primary years. Yet in the vast majority of primary-school settings, education in the arts is givenvery little time or left out altogether. For this reason it is especially important that parents encourage and support their children's art activities. Parents can help make the arts a central element of their children's experience.

In both kindergarten and first grade, variety is a vital element of the curriculum. In the best and most developmentally appropriate K–1 classrooms, teachers and children plant beans, raise gerbils, and hatch chickens; sort marbles, rocks, nuts, and bolts; bake cookies; play; learn nursery rhymes; sing songs; read hundreds of books; observe, think, question, label, and record; enjoy music and art; pay attention to nutrition; practice good citizenship; and think about values. All this is part of a conscious plan to lay a solid foundation for further learning.

Conversations with Your Child

This chapter presents an array of "conversation starters" for you to use with your kindergarten or first grade child. I use the term *conversation* broadly, to include both question-and-answer dialogues and a variety of games and activities. The conversation starters are grouped by subject matter: the language arts and the creative arts, math, science and health, and social studies. Within each subject area the ideas are ordered developmentally, starting with ideas suited to younger K–1 children and progressing to suggestions for older K–1 children. Most of the ideas and suggestions I offer are broad and open-ended, but some are as specific as "Can you name the four seasons of the year?" And many of the conversation starters can be adapted and expanded by imaginative parents (and children) for an almost infinite number of possibilities.

Some of the conversations that are introduced in this volume of the *101 Educational Conversations You Should Have with Your Child* series will recur in later volumes. In part this is because the schools curriculum often overlaps from year to year. But it also reflects the developmental character of learning—the same ideas are right for different children at different ages. And returning to the same conversations or activities a year or more from now will let you see how your child's knowledge and understanding have grown.

The conversation starters are a way for you to discover what your child knows and understands in relation to what is typically taught in the schools. You should remember, however, that the curriculum is not identical in every school; a gap in your child's learning may simply mean that that particular subject has not yet been introduced in the classroom. Be satisfied if your child can engage in *most* of these conversations, even with partial knowledge or limited understanding. You can always return to problem areas later on, as your child's mastery increases. But what about areas of learning that appear to be entirely outside a child's knowledge? A first grade child, for example, may appear to know very little about such directions as left and right, up and down, above and below, behind and in front, over and under. I do not believe this is a serious problem; parents themselves can help children with this kind of learning. But the parents might, nonetheless, ask the child's teacher, "What are you doing to help the children work with directions?" On the other hand, if a first grade child is not beginning to recognize words in print or shows little interest in print, the parents should certainly talk with the teacher, even as they spend more time reading to the child at home.

These ideas have been framed as conversational exchanges or playful interactions, not as daily quizzes. They are designed to promote interaction between parents and children. And because conversation does not flourish when questions lend themselves to simple answers "yes," "no," and "I don't know"—most of the questions and activities have an open-ended quality. Try not to make them seem like tests, or like some form of Trivial Pursuit. Instead, work them naturally into the time you spend with your child. The conversations should occur in a relaxed, comfortable context—at dinner, during a walk or a game, perhaps in relation to shared television programs or movies, or at some quiet time.

In a fundamental way, these conversations are educational opportunities. They allow you not only to reinforce what your child's teacher is doing but to expand the teacher's efforts, enriching your child's education. I believe that parents will, in the process of engaging in the conversations, realize more fully that they too are important and capable teachers. An additional benefit is that parents who take part in these exchanges will show their children that learning is a valuable activity, one that can provide pleasure and is worthy of respect.

The conversations are built around some important assumptions. I have assumed that parents

- Read to their young children daily.

- Listen to their children, respond to their questions, and engage them in ongoing conversations.

- Find opportunities to play with their children—physically active games as well as board games.

- Take walks with their children—around the block, through the parks, to a local playground.

- Take their children to the library, zoos, museums, and nature trails.

- Listen to records and tapes with their children.
- Let their children help them cook, wash the car, or rake leaves.
- Watch television with their children and discuss the content of programs with them.
- Share family stories with their children.

By interacting with their children regularly and naturally in the course of these and other activities, parents come to know a great deal about their children's growth as learners. The questions, activities, and ideas in this chapter will tell parents even more about their children—particularly about what their children are learning in school. As you go through these conversations, keep in mind that kindergarten and the first grade are foundation years. Children are just beginning to consolidate ideas and relationships. For example, children can be taught to recognize words in isolation—*cat, hat, sat, bat, hold, go*—but reading is more than knowing lists of words. And if children learn number facts—2+2=4, 4-2=2, 5+2=7, 7-2=5—but cannot use them for purposes they actually understand, math is not likely to become for them the fascinating subject it can and should be.

All-Purpose Conversation Starters

Many conversations between you and your child can arise spontaneously from day-to-day events. You can create numerous opportunities for such interactions in the following way:

- Looking at all the materials your child brings home from school, you will see a variety of things, including worksheets, word lists, classification exercises, writing samples, sculptures, paintings, and sketches. Ask your child about them. Say, "This looks interesting. Can you tell me how you did it?" or "I see you are learning to add numbers. What numbers do you know how to add. Have you learned any rules?" Remember to be supportive rather than judgmental. If your child does not regularly bring writing, drawings, constructions, or paintings home from school, you should be concerned.

- Observe your child at play. You will see that your child often acts out or imitates school activities, stories, things seen on television, and the actions and speech patterns of family members. Such acting out is an important part of the learning process. It also gives parents many starting points for conversations, through remarks such as "You really do like reading to your younger sister" or "You are really getting the hang of kicking that soccer ball."

By looking closely at what your child brings home from school and how your child acts out new knowledge or skills while playing, you can keep in touch with your child's education. These observations form a significant part of what you know about your child.

Certain questions that promote conversation between you and your child are versatile enough to apply in just about any situation. They may already be part of your repertoire. If not, start working them into your conversations. Use them often, but always—to repeat a point I made earlier in this chapter—use them patiently and naturally.

The questions are: "I wonder why that is?" "What do you think is happening?" "Is there any other way to do it?" "What if you tried it that way?" These questions and the many variations you can invent not only help keep dialogue going but also stimulate inquiry and discovery.

Language and the Arts

During the early years, children need to acquire confidence in their ability to read and write. The biggest key to effective reading and writing is exposure to a broad range of language uses; this is how children gain understanding of what language can do. The schools will contribute to this understanding through the stories teachers read, the records and tapes children listen to, and the many intentional elaborations of words and word meanings teachers provide. But the home is where language is most fully developed. Try to read a broad range of literature to your child: rhymes, poems, fables, folktales, classic stories, and biographies. Sing songs together and play games. Such experiences will make a critical difference in your child's development. In addition, call attention to things in newspapers and magazines, leave written messages around for your child, and make sure that your *own* literacy is evident.

Read a story to your child, then ask the child to tell the story back to you. This is essentially an effort to see what listening skills your child has developed. Is he or she able to relate the major elements of the story? Does he or she understand the story?

You should read to your child every day during these early, formative years. Your child's interest in the stories you read will tell you a great deal about his or her developing listening and comprehension skills. By sometimes asking your child to tell the story back to you, you not only observe the growth of these skills but also encourage two-way communication.

Using the basic format of one of the stories you read, write a story together with your child. You write the first line, have your child dictate the second line, and so on. This is another way of ascertaining whether your child understands story sequence and knows the connection between speech and writing. It is a way to begin the writing process.

The Mother Goose rhymes and stories contain wonderful imagery and interesting language. Ask your child what stories from Mother Goose his or her teacher is reading. Read them also at home. Children's favorites often include "Jack and Jill," "Little Boy Blue," "Jack Be Nimble," "Mary Had a Little Lamb," "Three Blind Mice," "Rock-a-bye Baby," and such folktales as "The Three Little Pigs," "Rumpelstiltskin," and "Jack and the Beanstalk."

Draw a picture together with your child; then each of you tell a story from it.

Directions are important for many areas of study. You can see how well your child understands right and left, up and down, in front of and behind, above and below, with several familiar games. Simon Says ("Put your right hand up," and so on) is filled with learning possibilities.

Following directions is a constructive way to learn the language of direction. Occasionally you can provide such tasks as "Can you bring me the red book? It is just to the left of the blue book." (Or to the right, or above, or below.)

See how well your child listens to and passes on information. Ask your child to remind his or her mother, father, brother, or sister of something.

It is important that children know the names of objects in their environment. You can gain insight into what your child knows by playing games. You might look at a photograph or illustration and say, "Let's find all the men, women, chimneys, windows, dogs, cats, flowers, streetlights, road signs, restaurants," and so on.

Give each other words, with the idea that you are to make up a story around the word. This is an interesting way to see what words your child is learning and how he or she understands them.

Play games based on words. For example, say, "I like a particular *red* object in the room. What is it?" You and your child take turns.

As you read a story to your child, occasionally ask, "What does that remind you of? What do you see in your mind?" Mental images are important to ongoing learning.

Practice discovering what we feel when we close our eyes and touch different kinds of things: smooth, rough, furry, coarse, rubbery, mushy, greasy, gooey, slippery, slushy, heavy, light. This lets you not only hear your child's growing language but also add new vocabulary words.

Read signs together as you go for walks: stop signs, street names, product signs.

Identify letters together: *A, B, C, D, E*. Ask, "How many can you pick out?" By the end of kindergarten your child will know most of the letters in the alphabet, if not all of them.

Say, "Let's see how many words we can think of that begin with *B*, with *D*, with *P*." You can also use "words that have the *oo* sound in them," "words that end in *T*," or anything else you think of. This game reinforces some of the language work being done in school and lets you see how well your child is hearing the various sounds—the components of words.

Write the letters of the alphabet together. You write *A*, your child writes *B*, and so on. Go from uppercase to lowercase.

Shopping provides many opportunities to learn language and math. For example, you might say, "Can you get me three cans of tomato soup?" Or two cans of pork and beans, or two boxes of cereal (name a particular cereal). Also see how many labels your child can read as you go through the store.

Teach your child something that was important to you as a child—a folktale, a particular nursery rhyme related to your cultural background, a song. Come back to it at various times to see how much your child retains and understands.

Say, "Let's think of all the things we know that are hard, soft, noisy, quiet, nearby, far away, very pretty, very ugly, very tall, very short."

Play a word association game. You start by saying a word; your child is to say the first thing he or she thinks of. Then your child gives you a word, and so on.

Aesop's Fables are popular in school as ways of teaching lessons about people and life. Read fables to your child and ask what he or she thinks they mean.

Listen to music together. Talk about how it makes you feel—like "just sitting," "dreaming," "dancing," "marching." Move together to music. This will help your child enjoy music and also let you watch your child's music awareness grow.

This is another language-expanding conversation, but it will also tell you how much your child knows about many aspects of the world. Say, "Let's tell each other all we know about pyramids." (Or rivers, bears, trees, birds, wind, numbers, bones, rocks, the sky, cities, outer space, cars, and so on.) You can see what words your child knows as well as introduce new words to your child's vocabulary.

Give your child a simple model of an airplane, boat, house, or car to put together, following the instructions that are given. (Such instructions usually have pictures as well as words.) How does he or she follow the directions? Does he or she seem to grasp what to do?

Ask your child to pick out all the words he or she recognizes as you walk through a mall or page through a children's book.

Use birthdays, holidays, or special family times as occasions for writing. Ask your child to write a letter to a grandmother, grandfather, or other close relative. Writing can be encouraged in lots of ways. For example, leave notes for your child and ask him or her to leave notes for you. When you read what your child has written, pay more attention to the ideas, the inventions, and the sustained stories than to spelling and punctuation.

When you are reading a story, ask, "What do you think will happen next?" How well can your child predict the progress of a story? Prediction is an important part of early reading.

Ask your child to bring home a favorite book from school to read to you; do this on a fairly regular basis. After your child has read the book, ask what he or she likes most about the story. As you listen to your child read the book, you will gain a good sense of your child's growth as a reader. Do not be alarmed if he or she skips a word occasionally, or reads "home" as "house." Is the story coherent and understandable as your child reads it? Is your child's reading fluent or is it halting, with long stops between words?

Look at paintings together, either at museums or in books and magazines. Van Gogh, Gauguin, and Picasso have a great deal of appeal to children. Ask your child what he or she likes in each painting. You will gain some insight into your child's growing understanding of color and into his or her imagination.

Say, "Let's think of all the things rain does." It falls, splashes, drops, makes puddles, and so on. Go on to wind, the sun, the moon, an animal, or any other noun that might suggest a variety of action words to your child.

Mathematics

Like language, math is a subject in which it is important for children to build confidence. In kindergarten and grade 1, the emphasis is on quantities, size, scale, and estimation. The more concrete the learning, and the more children are encouraged to see mathematics in use all around them, the better. You can help by using math and the language of math around the house. When measuring, have your child hold one end of the tape; talk about splitting apples into halves and quarters; describe activities in terms of order and sequence, using words like "first" and "second"; keep a growth chart of your child; use numbers aloud when you are counting things; make estimates and judgments about distance and time; play a lot of number-oriented games. Math is as natural as any other area of learning, and it should always be as interesting.

Cut out cardboard squares, triangles, and circles (five of each, at least two to three inches in size). Make a game of putting the shapes that are the same together. This is an exercise in classification. Does your child recognize the difference in the shapes? Does he or she know what the shapes are called? If not, ask again at a later time.

Put your cardboard shapes into a pattern: for example, line up a circle, square, triangle, circle, square, and triangle. Ask your child to put the other pieces together in the same pattern. This is another classification activity.

Put out five buttons and ask your child, "How many buttons are there?" Take two away and ask, "How many are there now?" You could add to this as a way of determining how your child's understanding of numbers is developing.

Another way of seeing how well your child understands numbers is to play board games that call for markers to be moved forward and backward so many spaces—for example, "Now you can move four spaces forward."

Ask your child to help you measure something in the house—a rectangular table, a room, a bookshelf. The process will demonstrate your child's beginning measurement skills.

With counters (buttons, game pieces, or the like) at hand, ask what two plus two equals, what two minus one equals, whether five is greater than four or less than four.

Telling time is an important skill. Occasionally ask your child, "Can you see what time it is?" (Do not expect a precise reading unless from a digital clock.)

While cooking or baking, ask your child to put in some of what the recipe calls for: three tablespoons of sugar, two cups of flour, and the like. This is a good way to see your child put math to use.

There are many opportunities for counting during everyday activities. While cooking you could ask, "Can you count out six potatoes?" Or ask, "Can you put ten cookies on the plate for dessert?"

Read the house numbers as you go around the block.

While you are getting ready for a walk, ask your child, "How long will it take us to walk around the block?" Questions like this arise in many different circumstances. The answers will show you how your child is coming to understand time.

From a handful of mixed coins, ask your child to pick out a penny, a nickel, a dime, and a quarter.

Ask, "If I gave you a dime and you bought something that cost a nickel, how much would the store person give back to you?"

Estimating weight is another way of exploring your child's growing powers of discrimination. Take two objects and ask, "Which is heavier?" or "Are they the same weight?" (Others in the family can get involved in this and other activities.)

Many games will reveal your child's knowledge of numbers— and also of words and directions. Try bingo, tic-tac-toe, dots, checkers, chess, concentration, hangman, Scrabble, chutes and ladders, and card games.

Measure each other's height: standing up, sitting down, kneeling, lying down. This is another activity that will give your child practice with measuring and also keep you informed about your child's progress.

The possibilities for measurement are endless. Try measuring the width of hands, the length of feet, the distance between outstretched hands, and the distance around the head or waist.

Make a two-part game of estimating and counting or measuring. First say, "I wonder how many steps it would take to get from the living room to the kitchen." After your child makes an estimate, you can count the steps together. Similar games might involve hand spans ("How many hand spans in the length of the table?") or weight ("How many leaves would we need to make a pound? How about marbles? Or pennies?").

Make up problems. For example: "It takes us 30 minutes to get to Uncle Jack's house. He wants us there by 6:00. When should we leave?"

Ask your child how you could make halves out of a piece of paper? How could you get four equal parts, or quarters?

Using a stopwatch, ask your child to tell you when a minute has gone by, then two minutes, then three minutes. Make a graph of your child's estimates over a week. Do they get more accurate? This kind of estimation can lead to such games as "How many words can I write in one minute?" or "How long does it take for my mother to read 'Jack and the Beanstalk' to me?"

With the stopwatch, see how quickly your child can run 20 yards.

Record and graph the times over several weeks. There is an almost limitless number of activities of this kind. You can also move into calculations such as "How fast did you go per second in feet? In yards?"

Count backward from ten to one with your child. You say, "Ten," your child says, "Nine," and so on. K–1 children learning to use numbers will be engaged in such activities in school.

Write numbers together. You write 1, your child writes 2, you write 3. See where it stops. You will get further as the months go by.

Use numbers to refer your child to interesting pictures in magazines or newspapers. Say, "There is a very funny picture on page seven."

Estimate with your child. Say, "Which pole is taller?" "Which house or building on the street is the tallest?" "Which child in the picture is the shortest?"

Computations of weight, size, and scale are important. You might pose such questions as "Which of these two objects is heavier?" (Or lighter, smaller, bigger, longer, shorter, thicker, thinner.) Also you could ask, "How can we be sure?" This leads your child to use his or her measuring skills.

See what math symbols your child knows. Ask about = (equals, the same as), - (minus, take away), + (plus), < (less than), and > (more than).

An ear of corn or a sunflower can provide an opportunity for estimating. Say, "How many kernels?" "How many seeds?"

Science and Health

Science study in the early years is mostly concerned with the natural world—wind and rain, ponds, the sky, animals and plants. Children observe nature and learn how things move through life cycles. The primary grades are a time to keep curiosity alive and to provide children with good skills in observation and problem solving.

Close observation is a primary objective of the science program. You and your child can examine a rock, a tree, a leaf, or an insect. Take turns asking, "What do I see?"

Observe cloud shapes together. Ask, "What shapes do you see in the clouds?"

Animals are part of the environment. You might ask your child to tell you the sounds animals make. "What do sheep say? Dogs? Cows? Cats? Birds?"

Much science education in school is related to sizes, colors, and shapes. You might ask your child to sort buttons by size (big and small), by color, or by shape. Objects can also be grouped by smooth or rough, soft or hard.

Animals provide opportunities to use the language of comparisons and relationships. Robins are smaller than _____, larger than _____. What do dogs and cats have in common? How are they different? What do birds have in common? How are they different? Are the feathers the same or different?

Walks afford many opportunities to identify objects in the environment. You can say, "What do you think that is?" "What kind of bird is that?" "Let's see how many different kinds of trees we can find in this block" (or park, or outdoor mall).

Children study parts of the body in school. Together you and your child can name various parts of the body: eyes, nose, ears, mouth, shoulders, arms, hands, fingers, toes, feet, legs, knees. You might also inquire about the heart, lungs, blood, and bones.

Ask why it is important to get exercise, to rest, to drink milk, to eat well. See what your child is learning in health.

Bring home a package of tomato seeds and suggest that your child plant them and see if they will grow. Notice how your child goes about it. Does he or she say, "Get some soil and a pot, put the seeds in the soil, water it, place it near the light"?

Science in school increasingly gives attention to the sources of common things and to everyday processes. You and your child can investigate questions such as "Where does our water come from?" or "Where does our sewage go?"

A question such as "How would we know which way the wind is blowing?" provides an opportunity for creative problem solving. Ask, "Is there any other way we could find out?"

Make a game of identifying sounds you and your child hear: wind whistling through the trees, water boiling, pots and pans banging, engines running.

Suggest making lists: "Let's think of all the animals [or plants] we can." Keep adding to the list over time and see how long it gets.

You might say, "Let's think of all the things you can do that the animals can't do."

Do simple science experiments with your child. For example, ask, "If I wanted to know how much the water in the jar weighs, what would I do?" Such experiments give a good indication of your child's thinking processes.

Observe birds in flight. Have your child demonstrate their flight patterns. Or observe spiderwebs and see if your child can draw them.

Examine a single tree. See what your child notices: the shape, the size, the texture of the bark, the colors of the leaves. You can make seasonal observations of the leaves at different stages or of the tree's fruits or seeds. Sketch the tree at different times of the year.

Watch nature programs on TV with your child. They offer opportunities for interesting conversations about new things your child has learned. Your child's level of interest, and the questions he or she asks, are a good indication of what the child is learning in school about nature.

Dinosaurs fascinate every young child. Ask your child if he or she is studying dinosaurs. (Do this at a time when you know that the answer is yes.) Ask your child, "What do you know about them?" "What did they eat?" "What happened to them?"

Children are also greatly interested in water; in the best K–1 classrooms children work a good deal with water. You could ask your child which of several objects (a cork, a penny, a piece of aluminum, a pencil, a crayon) will float and which will sink. Ask why the cork floats and the penny sinks. Your child will not know about density, but you will see how far he or she has developed the ability to formulate possible reasons for what happens.

Experiment with a magnet. Ask your child what it will attract and what it won't. Then have the child test it. Ask, "What are the rules for magnets?"

Ask your child to draw the solar system with as many planets as he or she can. The planets are typically discussed in K–1 classrooms, and this exercise will let you see what your child understands about the solar system. Try it at different times to see how the child's knowledge is growing.

The life cycle is a large element of primary school science; this is one of the reasons students keep mice and hamsters, hatch chicken eggs, and watch caterpillars turn into butterflies. It is also why many primary classrooms have made ties to senior centers and have invited mothers to bring their infants to class on occasion. See what your child has observed about baby mice, hamsters, chickens, or butterflies—or about human infants or older people. If he or she has questions, try to suggest ways of finding out the answers.

Social Studies

K–1 social studies are related principally to relationships within families and communities. But they also include aspects of geography and time; this is the basis for more formal studies in the higher grades. A child's work in social studies, as in the other subject areas, should be concrete and focused on what is visible in the world. Dramatic play is a good learning tool, as are many of the stories that are read to the children.

Watch a children's program such as "Sesame Street" or "The Electric Company" together. Ask your child to tell you what is going on.

Have your child talk on the telephone to Grandma or Grandpa, uncles and aunts. You will see how the child is gaining confidence and language skills.

As your child is learning the days and segments of days, you might ask, "What are the days in the week?" "What do we mean when we say morning, afternoon, evening, night?"

Look at photographs together. Family pictures showing you and your child at different ages are a good choice. Ask, "What can you remember about earlier times?"

It is important that your child be able to identify himself or herself. Have your child write his or her name and address.

Look at photographs of children in other parts of the world. See whether your child knows where these children come from. Ask how he or she knows.

Children typically learn the cardinal directions: north, south, east, and west. Ask your child where the sun rises. Ask where it goes down, or sets. Look at a map together. Ask, "Where is north? Where is south?"

Social studies in kindergarten and grade 1 covers basic geography. Children start to learn about maps and regions of the world. You might ask your child if he or she knows the two largest oceans. Also ask, "What is a desert?" "What is a swamp?" "What is a jungle?" "What are mountains?"

Ask what scientists, fire fighters, mechanics, pilots, lawyers, and farmers do. Take turns thinking of other jobs.

Ask, "What do we call the season of the year when it is very cold?" Or very warm, or when the leaves fall, or when the buds appear on the trees.

Ask your child, "What do you understand when I say 'A long time ago'?"

Children celebrate several different holidays in school. Thanksgiving, Presidents' Day, Martin Luther King, Jr., Day, and Columbus Day tend to receive the most attention, providing good opportunities to ask your child what he or she has learned about the Pilgrims, the Indians, George Washington, Abraham Lincoln, and Martin Luther King, Jr.

Ask, "What are some of the Indian tribes you have learned about?" "How did the Indians live years ago?"

See what countries your child has heard about other than the United States. Ask where these countries are and what the people who live there are like.

Ask your child to draw a picture of how a house is built, how a car is made, and so on. You will learn about your child's growing awareness of relationships and language.

Look at maps of your town or city with your child. Using the map, ask your child how to get to the library or some other landmark.

See if your child knows who the president of the United States is. How about the mayor of your town or city? The governor of your state? Ask what these persons do. You might also see what your child understands about voting.

Get in the habit of asking, "What do you think?" often. Listen carefully to your child's responses. This tells you a great deal about what your child understands. It also tells the child that his or her opinions mean something.

A sense of history is important to ongoing learning. You might ask, "Do you know how children lived years and years ago?" "What have you learned about that?"

Children hear a great deal about how we need to safeguard the environment and protect the world. Ask your child how we can keep the environment safe. Get a sense of what he or she understands about pollution, recycling, or rain forests.

The calendar is discussed a good deal in school. Questions such as "What month is it?" "Whose birthday is in October?" "How many days are there in September?" and "In what month does Valentine's Day fall?" are common. Ask your child, "What does a calendar tell us?" Make a game of naming the months.

Ask your child to teach you something he or she has learned in school.

6 Parents and Schools

As I said in the introduction to this book, parents are critically important to their children's education. By reading to their children daily during the preschool and primary school years, including them in family conversations, listening to them, providing them with varied experiences, and understanding that play and the exploration of diverse objects and environments are vital elements of learning, parents contribute greatly to their children's development and help make them into successful learners. Young children need the active interest of their parents. They need to see that their parents care about them and their learning. Further, children should know that their parents value language and are inquisitive about the world—that their parents, in fact, are also learners.

As the elementary years proceed, it is crucial for parents to continue reading to their children, sharing interesting stories from the newspapers and magazines as well as from the rich literature of mythology, biography, and travel. They should take walks with their children, making note of the environment and posing interesting questions along the way. Playing board games that demand problem solving, or watching television together and discussing the programs afterward are also ways to share in a child's learning while fostering a healthy relationship.

As children get older and move through middle school and secondary school, their interactions with their parents necessarily change. But parents' support remains important. Parents will find that taking an interest in what their children are reading and writing is an excellent starting point for conversations, no matter what age the children are. They will also discover that they can learn a great deal from their adolescent children, who may be reading literature or studying historical and scientific topics that the parents either never knew about or have forgotten.

The parents' partnership with the school is also important. Maintaining this partnership may seem easier and more natural when children are in the primary grades, but parents should consider it a priority throughout *all* the grades. In the best situations, teachers actively seek connections with parents. They call on the phone, write personal letters, and hold informal discussions. And they make certain that conferences are scheduled for times when parents are able to attend. If teachers do not do these things, then parents ask *why*.

Parents should expect their children's teachers to explain fully what the school year will be like, what topics will be studied, what problems are to be explored, what is to be read, what kinds of writing will be done, how the teachers will assess their students' progress, and how parents will be kept informed. If this information is not made available to parents, the parents should ask for it regularly.

To make the most of whatever information teachers provide, parents should try to spend some time—possibly a couple of days each year—in their child's classroom, especially during the early years. This gives parents valuable direct insight into what their children's educational experiences are like. It also helps them understand the intentions of their children's teachers, which makes interactions between parents and teachers more constructive.

Many teachers actively encourage parents to be classroom partners. Parents may share some of their own experiences, read to children, take small groups of children on field trips, and the like. A few hours each week for such participation is very useful to both parents and children.

How should parents approach their children's teachers and the schools? In most cases the teacher-parent exchange will be relatively easy. Teachers *want* connections with parents. They understand well the importance of parents as first and ongoing educators of their children. But they also know that parents have not always been sufficiently involved with their children or particularly responsive to teachers' efforts to interact with them. Both parents and teachers must strive for constructive, reciprocal exchanges.

Parents know their children. They know their interests and preferences, how they approach new situations, and how much they understand of the world. Parents need to share this knowledge with teachers in order to help the teachers be more effective. If your son or daughter is unhappy with school, feels unsuccessful or bored, seems not to be making progress as a learner, or is unable to take part in many of the conversations outlined on pages 43–68, make an appointment with the child's teacher. *This is an important first step.*

Your meeting with the teacher should not be confrontational or angry. There is no need for defensiveness or anxiety. Share your concerns in as natural a manner as possible. If you have sensed that your child is unhappy about school, the teacher has probably sensed this also. If you have noticed that your child has lost interest in reading, seems uninquisitive about the natural world, or appears vague about mathematics and its uses, the teacher has probably observed these attitudes too. Now is the time for you and the teacher to come together on behalf of the child. Together parents and teachers can figure out how to proceed. You might ask how you can be more helpful. Can the teacher suggest ways for you to enlarge the child's understanding of math, or science, or language? Also inquire about what the teacher will do. Establish a schedule for meeting again to determine what progress is being made, and *keep* the schedule. If you create and maintain a seriousness of purpose where the child's education is concerned, you have taken a vital step toward improving that education.

As I said at the beginning, this book is intended to bring parents, children, and teachers together in a productive exchange centered on school learning. Most children, being the natural learners they are, will make academic progress in school—but their progress will be far greater if their parents are actively involved.

The schools generally meet students' needs reasonably well, if not always well enough. But they will also do far better if parents join with teachers in an active partnership. *Your Child's Classroom* (p. 5) describes some of the qualities of a healthy school learning environment. An active partnership between parents and schools is necessary if such environments are to become the reality in all schools. Teachers should be supported in their desire for smaller classes in the early years, for a wide range of instructional materials, for strong arts programs. By providing such support, parents help their children and all children.

Books Parents Might Find Useful

Armstrong, Thomas. *Awakening Your Child's Natural Genius*. Los Angeles: J. P. Tarcher, 1987.

————. *In Their Own Way: Discovery and Encouraging Your Child's Personal Learning Style*. Los Angeles: J. P. Tarcher, 1987.

Bissex, Glenda. *Gnys at Wrk: A Child Learns to Write and Read*. Cambridge: Harvard University Press, 1980.

Burns, Marilyn. *The I Hate Mathematics! Book*. Boston: Little, Brown, 1975.

Caulkins, Lucy M. *Lessons from a Child*. Portsmouth, NH: Heinemann, 1986.

Children's Television Workshop Parents' Guide to Learning. *Kids Who Love to Learn*. New York: Prentice Hall, 1989.

Clay, Marie. *Writing Begins at Home*. Portsmouth, NH: Heinemann, 1987.

Gardner, Howard. *Frames of Mind: The Theory of Multiple Intelligence*. New York: Basic Books, 1983.

Goodlad, John I. *A Place Called School*. New York: McGraw-Hill, 1987.

Healy, Jane. *Your Child's Growing Mind: A Parent's Guide to Learning from Birth to Adolescence*. New York: Doubleday, 1987.

Kline, Peter. *The Everyday Genius: Restoring Children's Natural Joy of Learning*. Arlington, VA: Great Ocean, 1988.

Lappe, Frances Moore. *What To Do After You Turn Off the TV*. New York: Ballantine, 1985.

Maeroff, Gene. *The School-Smart Parent*. New York: Random House, 1989.

Papert, Seymour. *Mindstorms: Children, Computers, and Powerful Ideas*. New York: Basic Books, 1980.

Rosner, Jerome. *Helping Children Overcome Learning Difficulties*. New York: Walker, 1979.

Schimmels, Cliff. *How To Help Your Child Survive and Thrive in Public Schools*. New York: Revell, 1982.

Schon, Isabel. *Books in Spanish for Children and Young Adults*. Metuchen, NJ: Scarecrow Press, 1985.

Singer, Dorothy, et al. *Use TV to Your Child's Advantage: The Parent's Guide*. Washington, DC: Acropolis, 1990.

Stein, Sara. *The Science Book*. Boston: Little, Brown, 1975.

Taylor, Denny. *Family Literacy: Young Children Learning to Read and Write*. Portsmouth, NH: Heinemann, 1983.

Weitzman, David. *My Backyard History Book*. Boston: Little, Brown, 1975.

Wilms, Denise, and Ilene Cooper. *A Guide to Non-Sexist Children's Books*. Chicago: Academy, 1987.

Several Guides to Good Literature for Elementary School–Age Children

American Library Association. *Opening Doors for Pre-School Children and Their Parents*. Washington, DC: American Library Association, 1981.

Jett-Simpson, May, ed. *Adventuring with Books*. Urbana, IL: National Council of Teachers of English, 1989.

Lamme, Linda. *Growing Up Reading: Sharing With Your Child the Joys of Reading.* Washington, DC: Acropolis, 1985.

Lipson, Eden Ross. *The New York Times Parent's Guide to the Best Books for Children.* New York: Times Books, 1991.

Lorrick, Nancy. *A Parent's Guide to Children's Reading.* New York: Bantam, 1982.

Pollock, Barbara. *The Black Experience in Children's Books.* New York: New York Public Libraries, 1984.

Booklists

Each Spring, *Booklist*, the journal of the American Library Association, publishes a list of notable books for children, based on "literary quality, originality of text and illustrations, design, format, subject matter of interest to children, and likelihood of acceptance by children."

The Fall issue of *The Reading Teacher*, published by the International Reading Association, lists books children themselves select each year as "best books." (Available at no charge by sending a stamped, self-addressed #10 envelope to the Children's Book Council, 67 Irving Place, New York, NY 10003.)

The Spring issue of *Social Education*, published by the National Council of the Social Studies, lists books selected each year that "are written primarily for children . . . ; emphasize human relations; present an original theme." (Available at no charge by sending a stamped, self-addressed #10 envelope to the Children's Book Council, 67 Irving Place, New York, NY 10003.)

The Spring issue of *Science and Children*, the journal of the National Science Teachers Association, lists children's books selected annually for readability and science accuracy and interest. (Available at no charge by sending a stamped, self-addressed #10 envelope to the Children's Book Council, 67 Irving Place, New York, NY 10003).

VITO PERRONE is Director of Teacher Education and Chair of Teaching, Curriculum, and Learning Environments at Harvard University. He has previous experience as a public school teacher, a university professor of history, education, and peace studies (University of North Dakota), and as dean of the New School and the Center for Teaching and Learning (both at the University of North Dakota). Dr. Perrone has written extensively about such issues as educational equity, humanities curriculum, progressive education, and evaluation. His most recent books are: *A Letter to Teachers: Reflections on Schooling and the Art of Teaching*; *Enlarging Student Assessment in Schools*; *Working Papers: Reflections on Teachers, Schools, and Communities*; *Visions of Peace*; and *Johanna Knudsen Miller: A Pioneer Teacher*.